AF256148

This book belongs to

Sarah Epstein is a designer, illustrator and award-winning author happily creating in her colourful studio in Melbourne, Australia. She has a Bachelor of Design and has worked in creative industries for over 30 years. Visit **sarahepsteinstudio.com** to find out more about Sarah's artwork and books, and also find Sarah online here:

sarahepsteinstudio   sarahepsteinart

sarahepsteinstudio

Published by Fourteen Press, 2026
Melbourne, Australia

Cover and internal design: Sarah Epstein

ISBN 978 1 76370 355 1 (hardcover)
ISBN 978 1 76370 354 4 (paperback)
ISBN 978 1 76370 353 7 (ebook)

To find more of Sarah Epstein's artwork, visit:
sarahepsteinstudio.com

Collective Nouns of Australian Animals

Sarah Epstein

14 PRESS

What exactly is a collective noun? It's the name we use to describe groups of animals, people or objects. And in the animal kingdom these names can be as unique and delightful as the animals themselves.

But the English language is always evolving, and sometimes the group names change as well.

Some collective nouns can be traced back to medieval times, while others are more recent, meaning there is no definitive list to describe groups of animals. In fact, a number of the animals featured in this book have more than one collective noun, and many of the modern names are more playful than 'proper'.

If you've ever wondered what we call a group of possums, or bilbies, or platypuses, or even redback spiders, read on to discover the fascinating collective nouns of our Australian animals.

a **riot** of kookaburras

a
mob
of red
kangaroos

an
army
of green
tree frogs

a lounge of
blue-tongued
lizards

a parade
of echidnas

a pack of
dingos

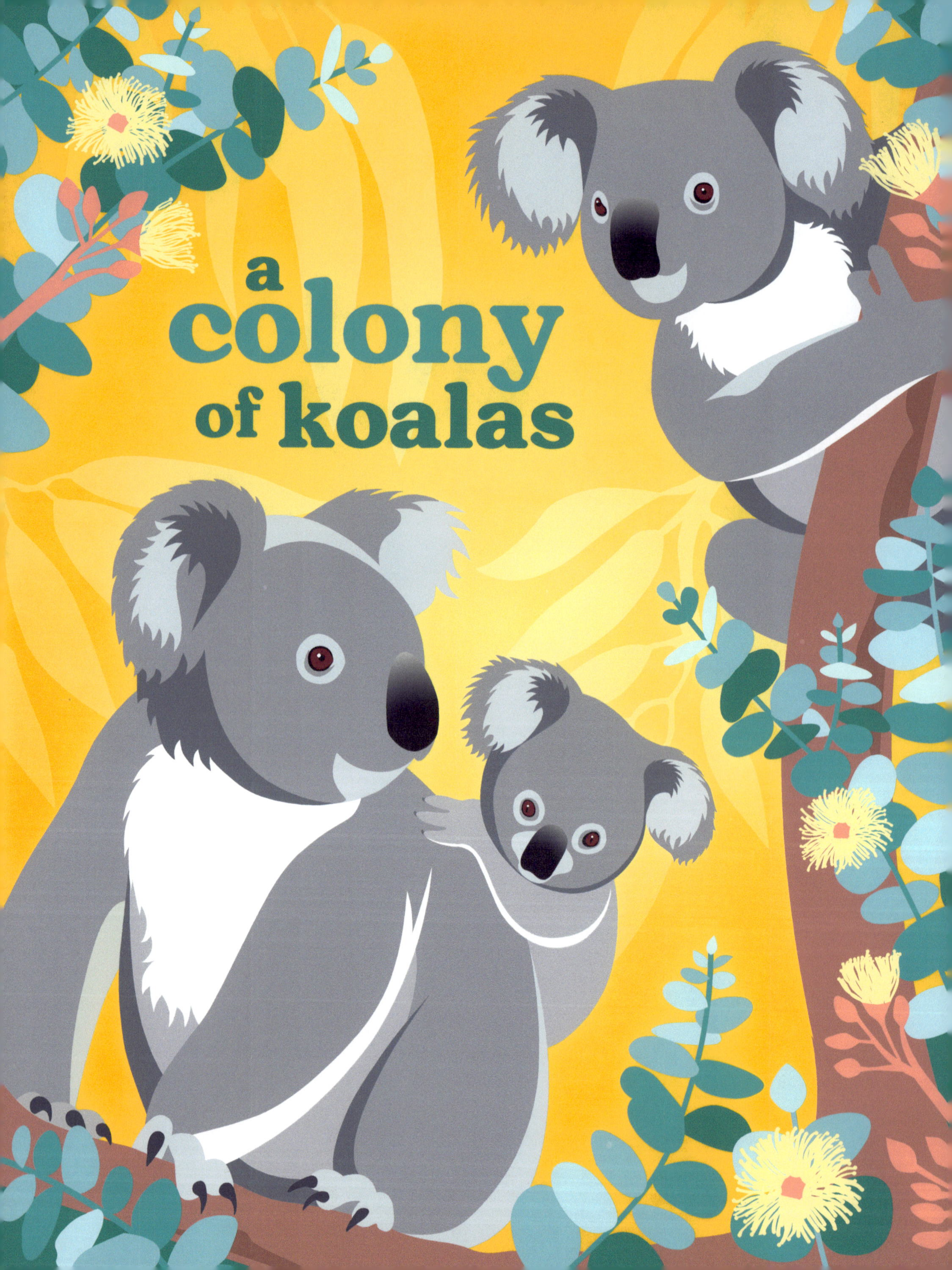
a
colony
of koalas

a bevy
of black
swans

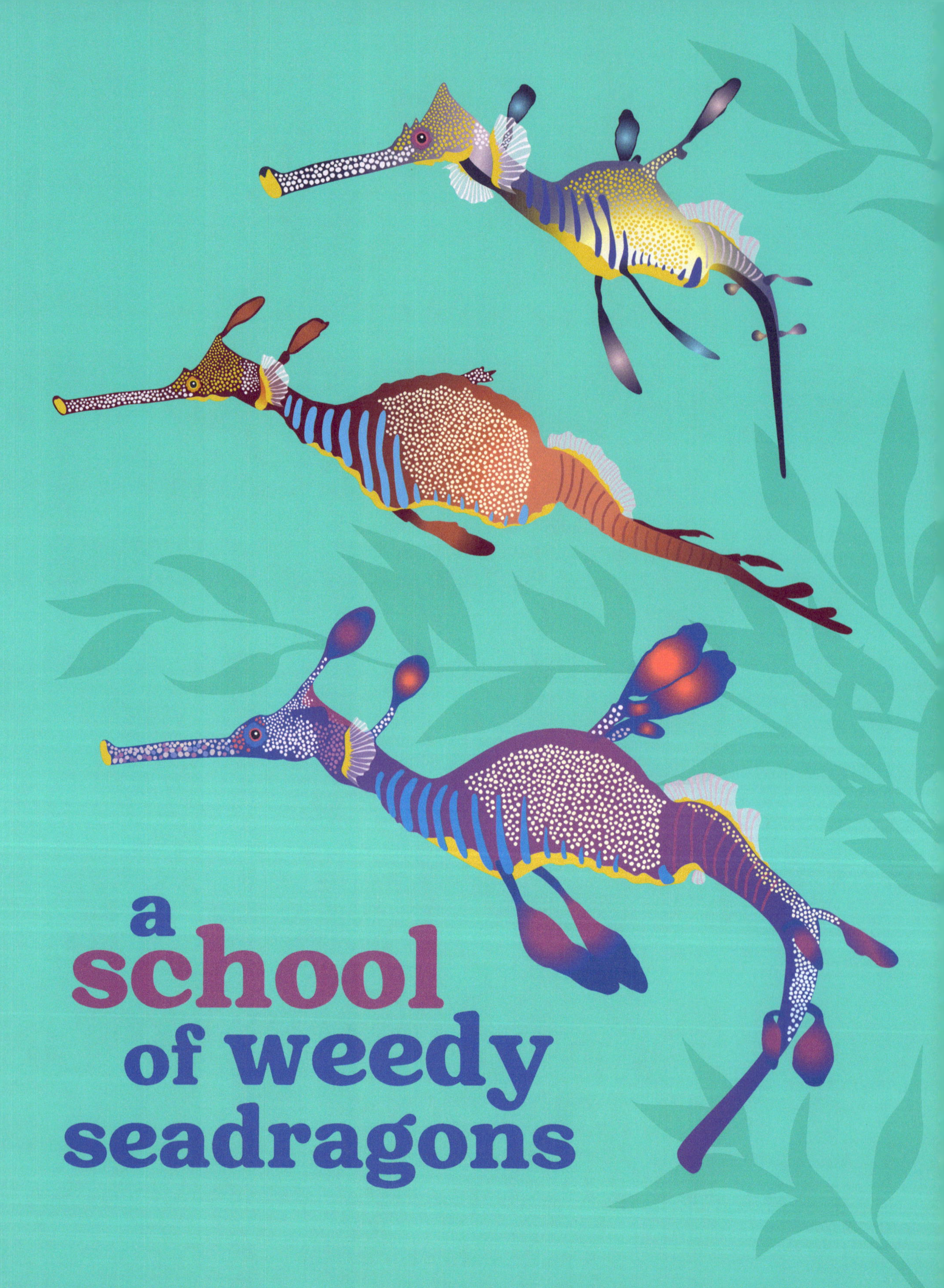
a school
of weedy
seadragons

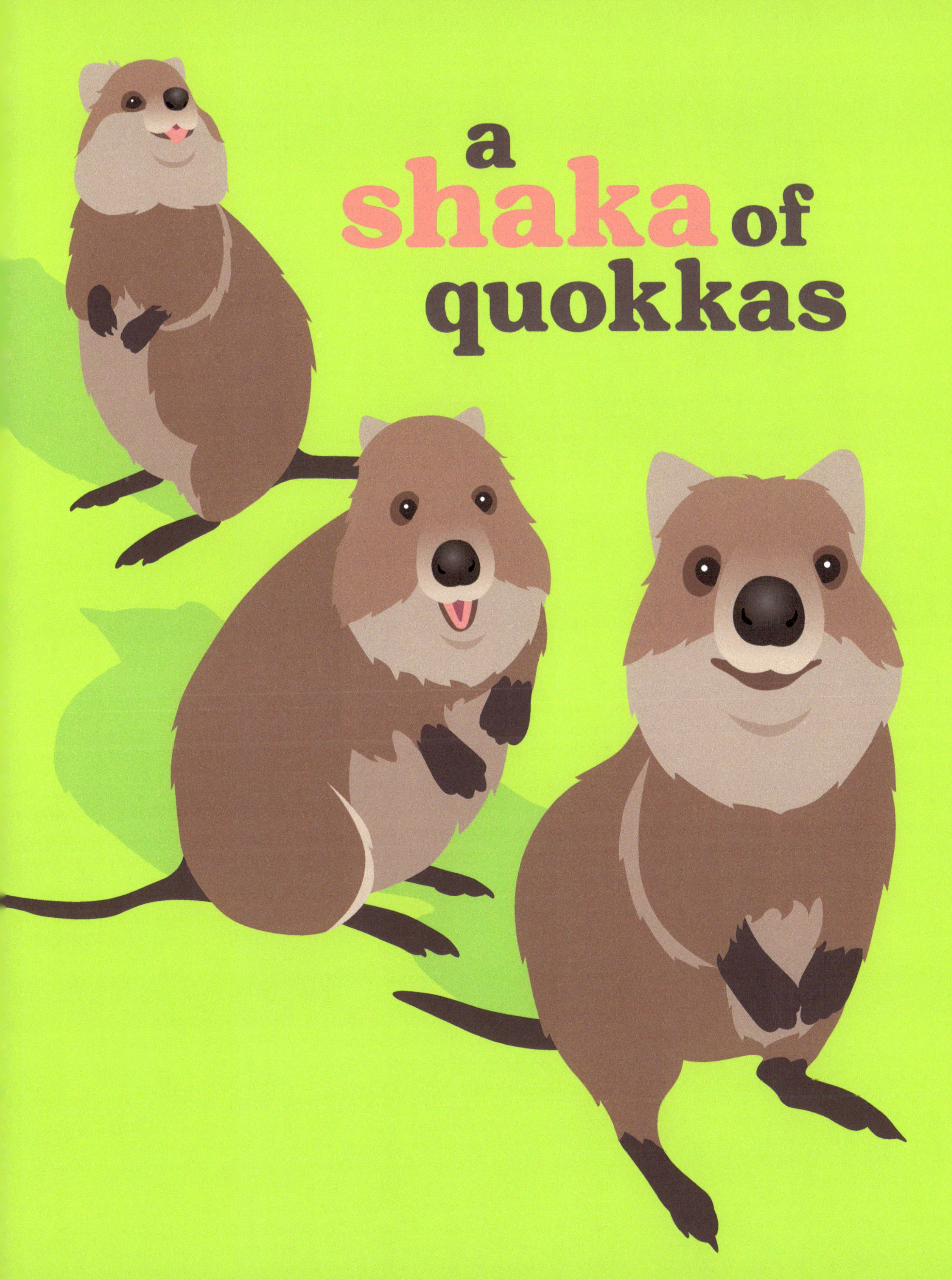
a
shaka of
quokkas

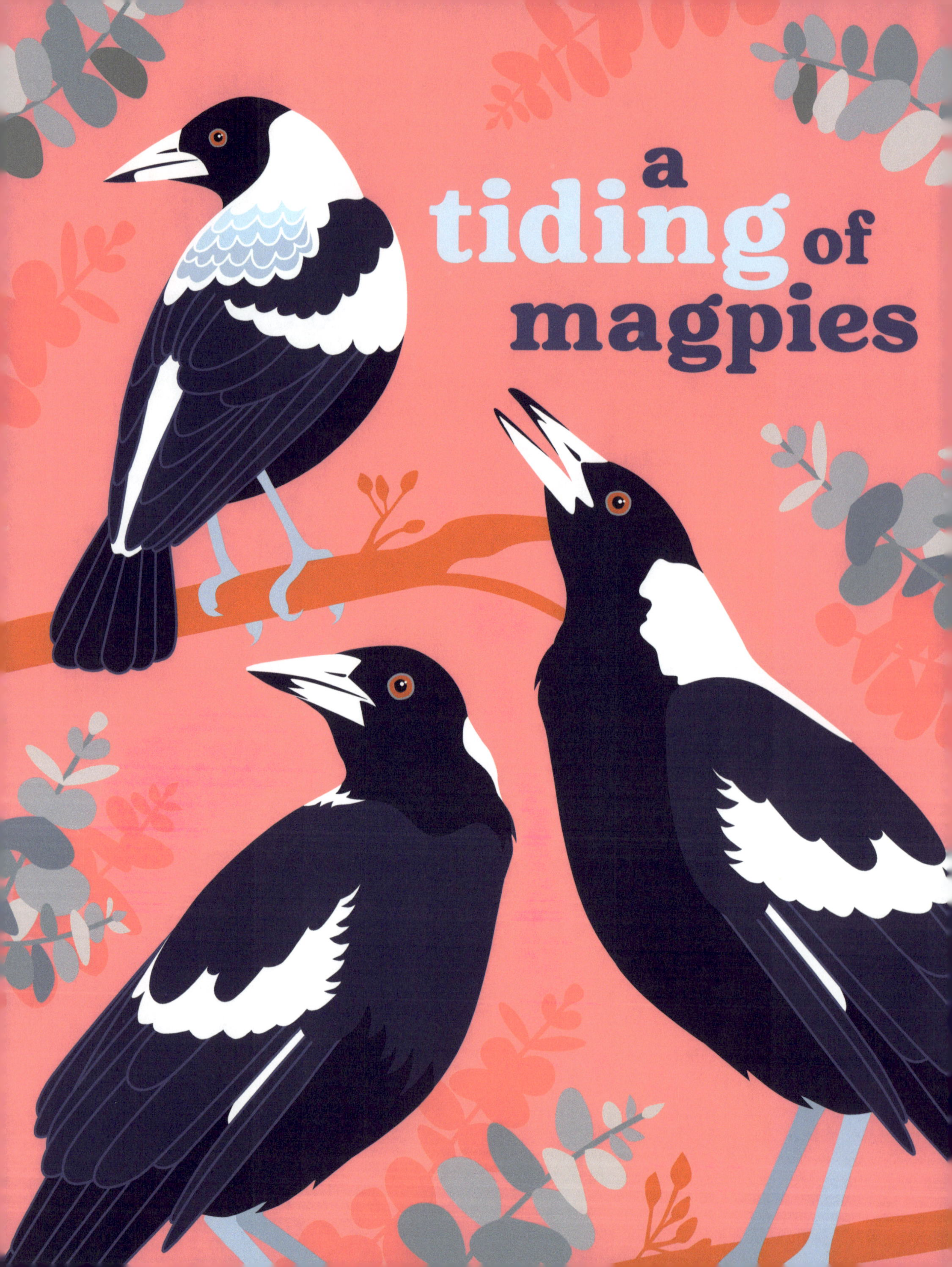

a tiding of magpies

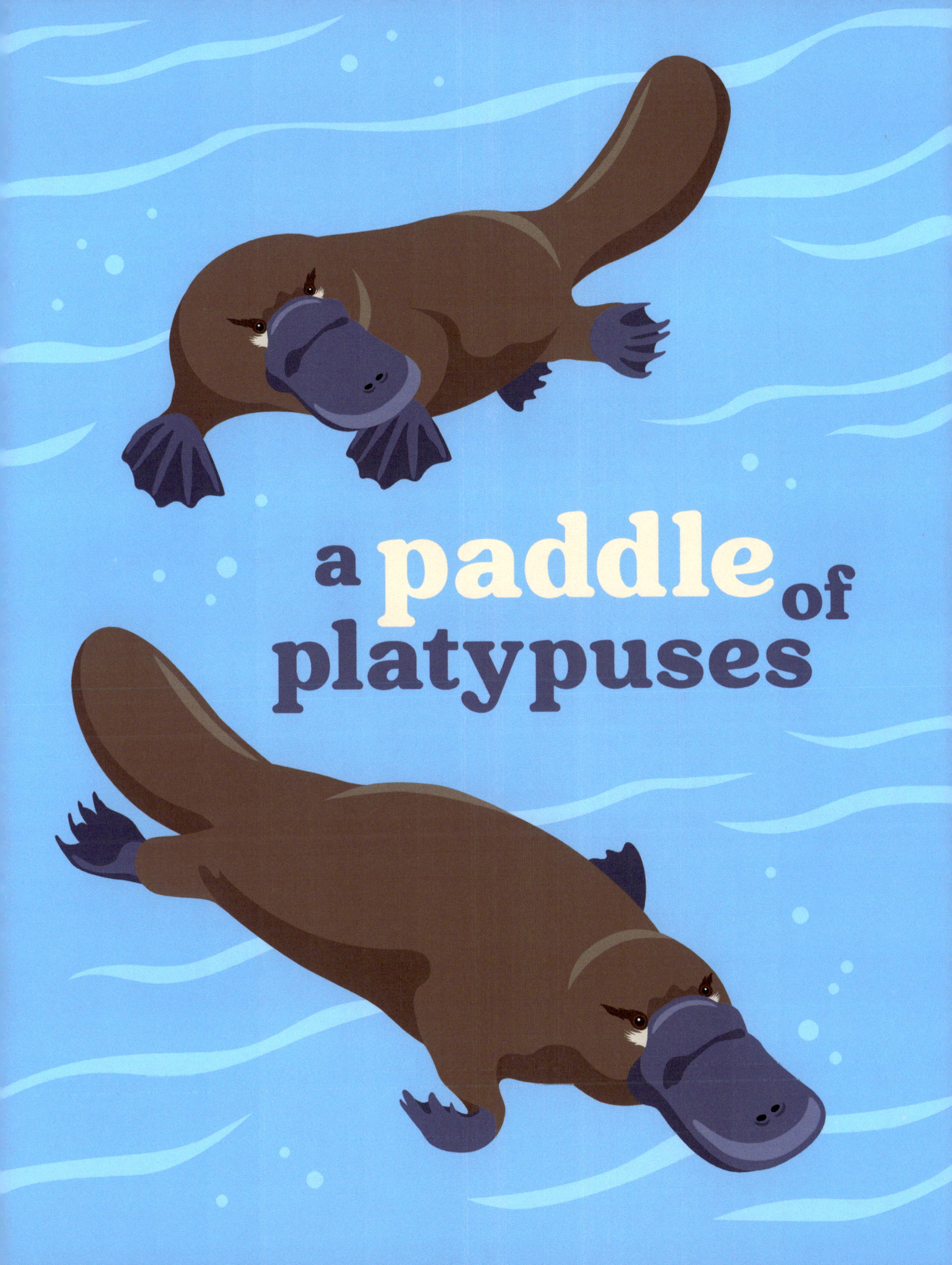
a paddle of platypuses

a bask of
crocodiles

a cluster
of redback
spiders

a
wisdom
of wombats

a
consortium
of blue-ringed
octopuses

a passel
of ringtail
possums

a crackle of
cockatoos

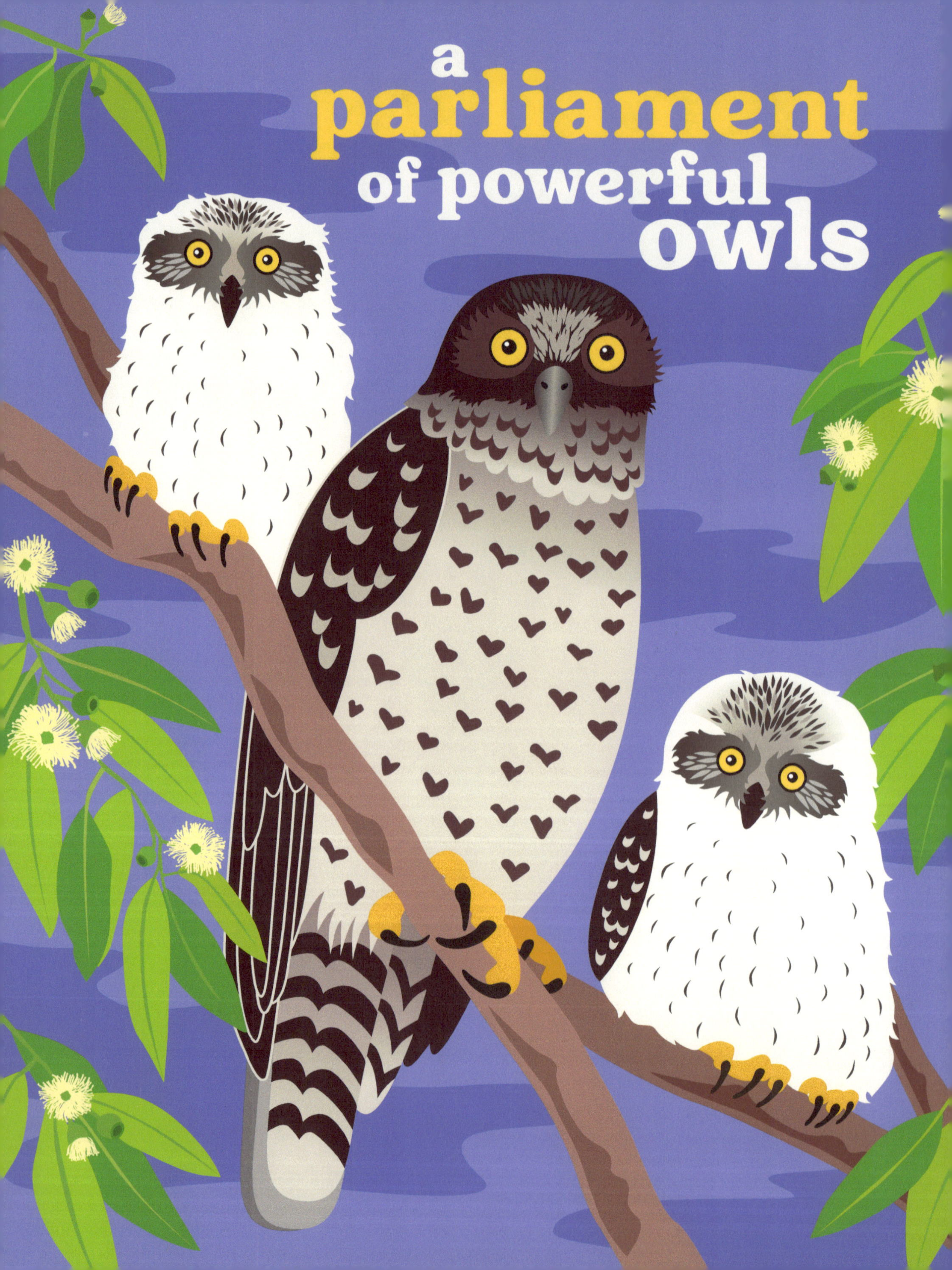
a parliament
of powerful
owls

a **smack**
of jelly
blubbers

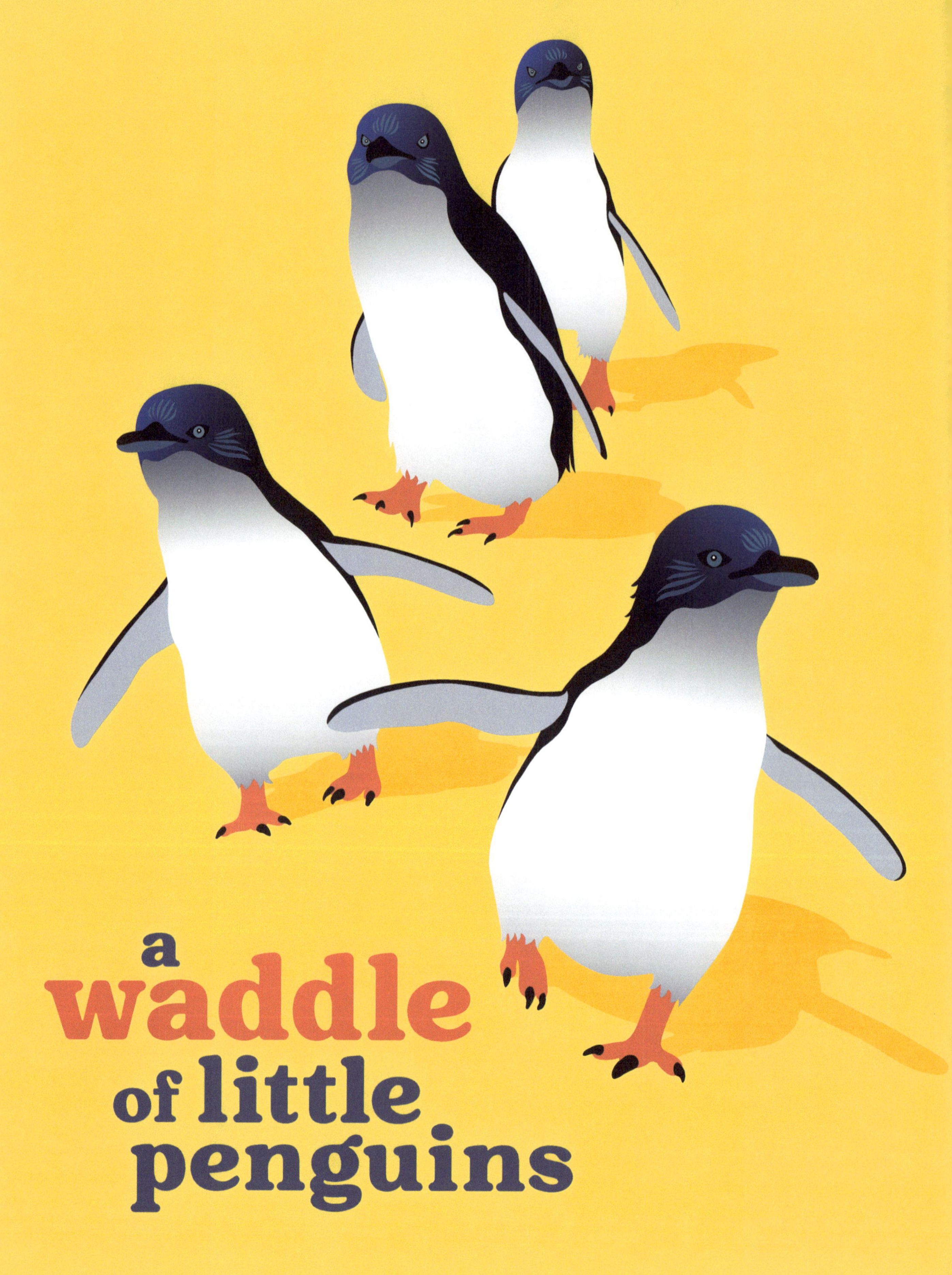

a waddle
of little
penguins

a
band
of
bilbies

a chatter of budgerigars

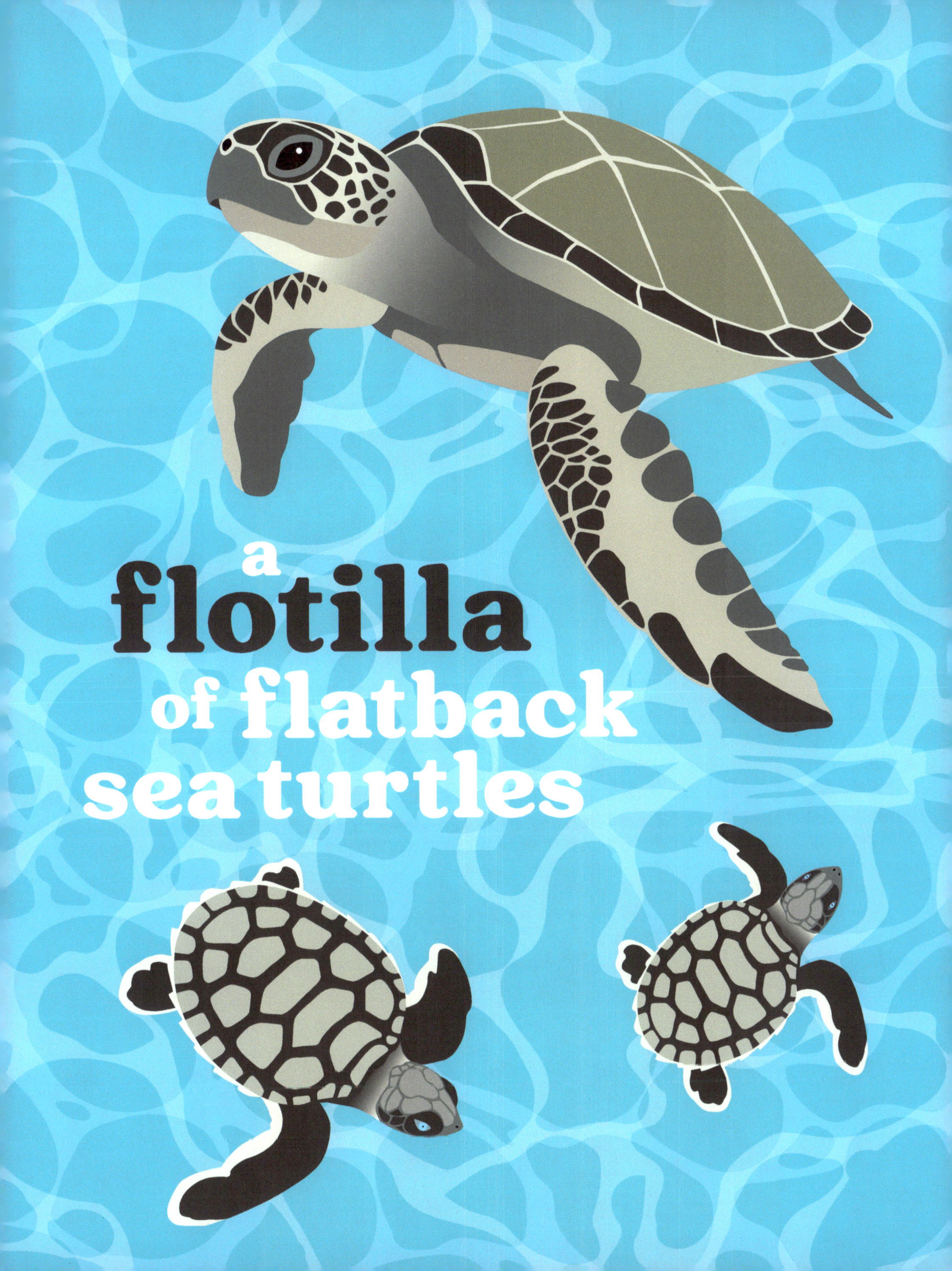
a
flotilla
of flatback
sea turtles

And what about Tasmanian devils?

They live very **solitary lives** and therefore don't have a **group name.**